SOCIAL INTELLIGENCE: A PRACTICAL GUIDE TO SOCIAL INTELLIGENCE

A BEGINNER'S GUIDE TO STRENGTHENING YOUR SOCIAL INTELLIGENCE TO BUILD RELATIONSHIPS AND BOOST YOUR CAREER

Why You Should Read This Book

Social intelligence is the most essential tool you require in order to reach your potential. It is the overarching pulse beneath how you speak to people, how people respond to you, how successful your interactions are, and, thusly, how successful you are in the world.

Therefore, a high social intelligence is all you need to live a wholesome, full, vibrant, and successful life.

But how do you build an appropriate level of social intelligence?

Certainly, we live in a world of lies, of dishonesty, of punishment, and of aggression. We live under the assertion that people who are the most aggressive, mean, continually ratcheted with furrowed eyebrows, will always get what they want because they want it the most—and they're willing to crush whomever they have to in order to get it.

But what if you could get what you wanted and become even more successful than this truly mean person who leaves a trail of hatred and anger behind him? What if social intelligence paved the path toward greater balance between you and your peers, fueling everyone with success and positivity, while also allowing you to achieve what you want?

Fuel yourself with social intelligence, this earnest ability to "work a room" without any negativity, with feelings of empathy, and with an earnest ability to speak to anyone about anything. Become the type of person people yearn to follow. Become the best version of a leader—the type of person that fuels an environment of respect, of creativity, of bolstered confidence, and of motivation.

Learn the steps to bring heightened social intelligence into your brain. Learn that social intelligence is much like any other muscle in your body. It must be worked—and worked well—in order to grow and allow you to meet your potential. Learn to fuel yourself with social intelligence so you can pass that understanding on to both your peers and your children. Your children will grow into empathetic, wholesome individuals who understand both themselves and others. This fuels a future of greater understanding, of heightened knowledge, and of growth.

Live a socially intelligent life. Learn to grow and develop in your relationships and in your career. Reach the peak of your motivation, and succeed in new heights.

TABLE OF CONTENTS

CHAPTER 1. WHAT IS SOCIAL INTELLIGENCE?

Social intelligence is the path to greater success and greater confidence.

But what, exactly, is it?

Let's begin with the following questions:

1. Do you find yourself getting along well with others often, easily falling into easy conversations with people you don't know?
2. Do you find yourself fitting in naturally with large groups of people, many of whom have different view points than you, have alternate ideas, or are all from different backgrounds?

If the answer is yes, then you probably have something called "social intelligence."

Social intelligence is the general ability to ease into environments of many different people. As you do this, these people not only accept you. They also work well with you, listen to you, and respond to what you have to say. Note that, on its most simplistic level, social intelligence is referred to as "people skills." But it is so much more than that. Look to the following points to better understand the intricacies of social intelligence.

1. Social intelligence brings you overarching awareness of social situations. Therefore, it's like you speak the "undercurrent" language of the social situation.

2. Social intelligence brings you awareness of the social dynamics in certain social situations. Therefore, you understand who the "dominant" person at the party is; you understand who is shy or reserved. You know who the popular people are, and you know who is not as welcome. You can "read the room," so they say. You are not lost.

3. Social intelligence brings you information about the strategies and styles involved with interacting with these people. This ability will give you heightened appeal at these social functions. You can speak to whomever you want or need to in a manner they would like and respond well to.

4. Social intelligence brings you an idea of how other people perceive you. Therefore, you understand how people will react to what you say and how you say it. You can alter your style to fit the style of the room. For example, you wouldn't speak loudly at a nursing home, and you wouldn't speak conservatively at a nightclub.

THE SOCIAL INTERACTION SPECTRUM

According to a researcher named Karl Albrecht, the behavior you have in a social situation ranks somewhere on a spectrum between a "nourishing" social effect and a "toxic" social effect. Note that this "toxic" action is something that makes other, surrounding people feel disrespected, guilty, angry, or somehow "less-than."

Note, then, that the "nourishing" social action is something that makes others feel affirmed in their sense of self, happy, intelligent, or otherwise valued in some way. Naturally, you're aiming for this nourishing social action.

Therefore, if you find that you have continual toxic effects in social interactions, you might have a low sense of social intelligence. You cannot connect with others; you cannot make your words influence other people on a strong, impactful, and appropriate level to ultimately reach a connection.

If you have a continued nourishment as a result of your behavior, however, you have a much more effective strategy in speaking with your peers. Therefore, you have a high social intelligence.

IS SOCIAL INTELLIGENCE AN ASPECT OF YOUR PERSONALITY?

According to the theory of multiple intelligences created by Harvard University's Professor Howard Gardner, social intelligence is an aspect of a group of intelligences, rather than an aspect of your personality. Alongside this comprehension, according to this theory of multiple intelligences, your "IQ" score is completely invalid. One number can't comprehend many different spheres. In fact, intelligence has many different spheres, many different dimensions that continually alter and change based on challenges and experiences. Therefore, your intelligence is much more like a muscle than anything else. It can be exercised. It can grow. As such, your social intelligence can grow with expert work.

There are six aspects or spheres of intelligence, according to Harvard's Howard Gardner. Find them listed below:

1. Intelligence Sphere of Abstract Abilities, which deals with verbal manipulation, conceptual

reasoning, mathematical abilities, and information about symbols.

2. Intelligence Sphere of Social Abilities, which deals with all successful social interactions with all people in all contexts. Note that this is the sphere of social intelligence.

3. Intelligence Sphere of Practicality, which deals with all problem-solving abilities based in common sense.

4. Intelligence Sphere of Emotional Abilities, which deals with an interior ability to mange and regulate your reactions post life experiences.

5. Intelligence Sphere of Aesthetic Abilities, which deals with your appreciation and adoration for beauty, for design, and for form. This element brings your love for art, music, and movies.

6. Intelligence Sphere of Kinesthetic Abilities, which deals with your ability to control your body through any activity, like singing or dancing, driving a car, etc.

THE MEASUREMENTS OF SOCIAL INTELLIGENCE

How does one measure social intelligence?

Essentially, social intelligence is measured through the identification and "measurement" of various important interaction skills.

After each interaction, these interactions skills are assessed with regards to the context of the interaction. Note that all person-to-person interaction occurs in the midst of certain contexts. Every conversation takes place in a certain light, as a result of something that has happened before or is currently happening. Think, for example, how different the conversation would have to be if it was taking place at a rock concert. Think how different it would be if it were occurring immediately after your divorce. Therefore, the importance of social intelligence is understanding and noting these contexts, taking them into account through all interactions.

THE DIFFERENCE BETWEEN SOCIAL INTELLIGENCE AND EMOTIONAL INTELLIGENCE

The above six spheres of intelligence lists both emotional intelligence and social intelligence as two different spheres, encapsulating different aspects of your actions and processes. However, many people attempt to list social intelligence processes alongside emotional intelligence processes, bringing "people skills" into the concept of understanding one's own emotions.

It is more appropriate to think of social intelligence as a separate but complimentary element with regards to emotional intelligence. Both are required in order to comprehend what's going on inside your own brain and utilize that interior to monitor the exterior interactions we have with other people. Note that if you struggle in certain aspects of social intelligence, this could be as a result of a lower quality of emotional intelligence. Furthermore, if you become unsuccessful in some aspects of social intelligence, you might feel "less-than" in your social intelligence, which can thus make you feel a lower sense of self. This involved emotional intelligence because you're allowing a negative reaction to take place on an interior level.

THE SOCIAL INTELLIGENCE PROFILE

The social intelligence profile works to identify social intelligence through three different perspectives. Each perspective works to bring a different portrait of social interaction that can yield the overall picture of your personal social intelligence "score."

Two of these perspectives come directly from you. They allow you to both judge and evaluate yourself after each interaction.

The third perspective yields your personal description of the style in which you interacted. This cannot be evaluated or judged. Rather it is a matter of personal preference. (How, exactly, you choose to interact with people. It is as personal as how you dress, how you wear your hair, or what you do for a living.)

THE FIRST PERSPECTIVE: SOCIAL SKILLS, VIA THE SPACE FORMULA.

This first perspective brings five basic behavioral categories:

SITUATIONAL AWARENESS

> This is your overall ability to note the context or the environment of the situation in which you're interacting. It involved your comprehension of how the situation is altering both your behavior and the behavior of others.

PRESENCE

Presence involves what kind of message you're yielding to other people as you speak, as you move, as you listen. This presence brings these other people understanding of who you are, how you feel about yourself, and your overall intelligence.

AUTHENTICITY

Authenticity brings the understanding of how honest other people believe you to be through your interaction with them. Therefore, do they think you are speaking to them with ethical motives? Do they think you're being honest? Do they think that everything you're doing aligns well with your interior values?

CLARITY

Clarity involves your abilities to say and express everything you're thinking and feeling in an effective and impactful manner. This brings an enhanced sphere of communication, involving listening, providing feedback to what you hear, paraphrasing what you hear, holding skill in how you choose your words, holding continuous flexibility in the semantics of what you're saying, and having the ability to say things clearly and concisely. Clearly, there is so much involved with clarity, it's no wonder we're so often lost and confused mid-conversation. It's no wonder there are so many ill-perceived interactions between humans.

EMPATHY

Empathy involves the ability to build links or connections with other people. This allows you to bring people on the same level of respect. They are willing to cooperate with you because they respect you and know that you respect them on the same level.

Through these five elements of your social interactive, you are meant to "judge" yourself. Try doing the following. Rank each of the previous five elements of your interaction from 1 to 5. 1 means that the specific element of your interaction was "toxic." Therefore, you didn't deliver an appropriate reaction given the context of the conversation. 5 means that this specific element of your conversation went incredibly well, that it was undeniably nourishing.

Note that the top level is 25. Therefore, if you rate between 20 and 25, you have incredibly nourishing social interaction. If you're between 15 and 20, you have a bit of work to do, but you still, generally speaking, get your point across, orchestrate an appropriate conversation, and exit the scenario unscathed. Between 0 and 15, however, finds a stark level of conversational abilities. You need to begin to assess how you can articulate yourself more clearly, how you can better empathize with your surroundings, how you can seem more "honest" when delivering a message to the person you're speaking with, and how you can generally understand or "read" the room in which you're speaking.

THE SECOND PERSPECTIVE: THE SELF-INSIGHT

This is the second essential element of your social intelligence profile. Through the self-insight element, you are meant to look at a series of pairs of adjectives, each of which are the exact opposite of their pair. Therefore, you might look at words such as: "cold and warm," or "long-winded and concise." As you peruse this list of contrasting adjectives, you are meant to articulate a number between 1 and 5 between these two words to express how others might see you when you speak to them. Therefore, you are meant to ask yourself if others perceive you as being "long-winded" or more concise. Are you somewhere in the middle? When you begin to look at these adjectives and diagnose the way you speak and the way you present yourself, you can begin to adjust how you present yourself and influence others.

THE THIRD PERSPECTIVE: YOUR PERSONALIZED INTERACTION STYLE

Note that every person has a specific style he utilizes when engaging in conversation. During this third perspective, you are meant to diagnose your specific style. Generally speaking, there are four primary options for your behavior. However, beyond these four primary options, there are two essential dimensions: your social energy and the focus of your results (post-conversation).

Social energy is your interior need to interact with other people, to influence other people, and to be influenced by other people. You either have a high social energy or a low social energy.

"The focus of your results" element means that you have a preference of getting things done through your own effort or through other people. Therefore, you either want to be the master of your domain, or you want other people to do things for you.

These two variables offer two extremes. You either have high social energy or low social energy, and you either have people focus or task focus. This allows the following four primary behavioral preferences that diagnose a large range of situations.

1. DRIVER

If you are the driver, you are task-oriented and you have a high social energy. Therefore, you utilize your high social energy in order to create the end results of your own tasks. You don't rely on others. An example of a driver is found with a person who is a leader who does not require the people to do anything to execute an end result.

2. ENERGIZER

If you are the energizer, you have a high social energy, but you are people oriented. Therefore, you utilize your high social energy in order to get people up and moving, get people going to do the tasks you think are important. An example of a good energizer is found with someone who is a leader of a club. These people utilize high energy to get everyone to go to meetings, do the same things together, and articulate an end goal.

3. LONER

A loner has low social energy and is further task oriented. Look to Gandhi for an example of a loner. He had strong beliefs, but he didn't have the strong, high energy to yell those beliefs to the people. Instead, he orchestrated his beliefs firmly, in a lonely manner. Eventually, people were motivated to follow him.

4. DIPLOMAT.

A diplomat is found with someone who has low social energy but who is further people-oriented. Therefore, he utilizes his low social energy to comprehend what the people need to do to better themselves and the greater society.

THE IMPORTANCE OF SOCIAL INTELLIGENCE

The importance of learning social intelligence lies in relationships. When you learn social intelligence, you boost both your social and communication skills. You allow yourself to create an effective dialogue with your friends, your family, and your colleagues.

Note that in this ever-evolving world, social intelligence is faltering. We interact with people fewer times today than ever before. Instead of going to meet friends for coffee, we text them or message them. We like what they put on Facebook. We don't have a dialogue that encapsulates all the nuances of communication. As such, we lose something along the way.

Note that social intelligence helps boost self-exploration and expression. It reduces bullying in schools, and it decreases the risk of misunderstandings amongst peers.

Furthermore, social intelligence at the home level is the most important of all. Partners and married couples must learn to communicate effectively to reach a level of equality and companionship. Children must have the ability to listen to their parents while still demonstrating the things they need in their lives. Harmony must exist at this household level, and this can only be achieved through social intelligence.

When you embark into the world as a college student or as a post-college student, looking for work, social intelligence further plays a mighty role in job interviews and excelling in any given career.

Because the Internet is such a stronghold in our lives, we must learn social intelligence for a variety of reasons. Through social intelligence, you can:

1. MANAGE YOUR RELATIONSHIPS.

This is perhaps the most essential element of social interaction, especially when it comes to the relationship between parents and teenagers. Essentially, through relationship management, teenagers must be able to handle both their problems with their parents and their problems with peers at school in an appropriate, mature manner. Furthermore, parents must be able to approach their children with social intelligence. They must respond appropriately to their teenager's (surely overdramatic, hormone-ridden) feelings. Note that parents should have empathy for their teenagers and what they're going through. They must learn to relate to them on some level in order to create an environment of trust.

2. UNDERSTAND YOURSELF ON AN INTIMATE LEVEL.

When you understand your unique perspective, you can speak to yourself through "self-talk" and comprehend what you really want in life and how you can get it—without shoving anyone to the side. You cannot approach any conversation, any relationship, without an appropriate sense of yourself.

3. HAVE AN ABILITY TO MANAGE YOUR CONFRONTATIONS.

When conflicts do occur—as they so frequently do—it is important that you hold appropriate social skills to manage these conflicts. You must make appropriate decisions with regards to what people are saying to you or what people are doing to you. You can utilize internal intuition to localize your emotions and not act "crazy" in the event of "attack." You must proceed with assertiveness, with control, and with empathy to halt the confrontation.

Naturally, there are many, many reasons that social intelligence is incredibly important. Proceed to the next section to get a better feel for where the science of social intelligence has been and where it is now. The field has grown exponentially.

CHAPTER 2. THE HISTORY OF SOCIAL INTELLIGENCE

According to Harvard University's Professor Howard Gardner:

"THE CAPACITY TO KNOW ONESELF AND TO KNOW OTHERS IS AS INALIENABLY A PART OF THE HUMAN CONDITION AS IS THE CAPACITY TO KNOW OBJECTS OR SOUNDS, AND IT DESERVES TO BE INVESTIGATED."

Nearly a century ago, in the year 1920, researcher E. L. Thorndike traced a line between social intelligence and both abstract and mechanical human intelligence. (Previously, they had all been incorrectly grouped together in the same sphere of intelligence.) He stated that the initial definition of social intelligence was the following: "the ability to understand and manage men and women, boys and girls—to act wisely in human relations."

After his initial statement, the term social intelligence was accepted into the psychological community. During this time, research was formulated in the scientific arena attempting to discover how people judge others, how accurate those judgments are, and what people consider good characteristics versus bad characteristics—and how accurate their assumptions are. Much like it is today, the main unit of measurement was rating one's self and answering many questionnaires.

During 1933, a researcher named Vernon expanded on the initial definition, stating that social intelligence also included "an ability to get along with people in general, social technique or ease in society, knowledge of social matters, susceptibility to stimuli from other members of a group, as well as insight into the temporary moods or the underlying personality traits of friends and of strangers."

THE FIRST STANDARD SOCIAL INTELLIGENCE TEST

The initial standard social intelligence test was founded in 1927. It was given the name The George Washington Social Intelligence Test. It brought about many subtests to articulate a wide variety of subsections of social intelligence, including:

1. Judgment of Social Situations
2. Observation of Human Behavior.
3. Memory for Names and Faces.
4. Recognition of Mental States from Facial Expression
5. Recognition of the Mental States Behind Words
6. Sense of Humor
7. Social Information

After initial work in the field of George Washing Social Intelligence, interest in social intelligence fell away until the 1960's. During this time, a man named Guildford created a Structure of Intellect model. According to this model, which he stated was based on the initial intelligence proposition by E. L. Thorndike, the first discoverer of social intelligence, social intelligence is represented with thirty different behavioral operations.

After this time, Guildford and another man named O'Sullivan worked to create tests of behavioral cognition. Prior to these tests, they went in with the assumption that "expressive behavior, more particularity facial expressions, voice inflections, postures, and gestures, are the cues from which intentional states are inferred." Therefore, they assumed that people infer how other people are feeling—or what the general context of the conversation is—through voice and facial cues. The researchers utilized cartoons, photographs, tape recordings, and drawings in order to understand how people both reacted to what they saw and heard and comprehended what the emotion behind each unit was.

The researchers developed the following six units of cognitive abilities as a result of the studies:

1. COGNITION OF BEHAVIORAL UNITS.

This described the ability to articulate the mental state of each person.

2. COGNITION OF BEHAVIORAL CLASSES.

This described the ability to associate many different people's mental states, whether or not they were similar, etc.

3. COGNITION OF BEHAVIORAL RELATIONS

This described the ability to understand the link between different behaviors.

4. COGNITION OF BEHAVIORAL SYSTEMS.

This described the ability to understand the appropriate order of social behaviors.

5. COGNITION OF BEHAVIORAL TRANSFORMATIONS.

This described the ability to respond and alter when the context or behavior changes in social interactions.

6. COGNITION OF BEHAVIORAL IMPLICATIONS.

This described the ability to comprehend what could come next in a particular social situation.

Guilford and O'Sullivan developed many social intelligence tests with regards to these structures. During one such study, they brought together 306 students of high school age. They all took twenty-three social intelligence tests that coincided with these hypothesized comprehensions of social intelligence.

Both Guilford and O'Sullivan created enormous efforts in the field of social intelligence. However, it's essential to remember that they only constructed a path that brought us partway toward understanding social intelligence on an intelligible level.

THE ELEMENTS OF SOCIAL INTELLIGENCE TODAY

After continued efforts in the field of social intelligence, psychological researchers have reached the following six elements of social intelligence. We've come a long way since that initial day when Thorndike ripped social intelligence from the rest of the intelligences and understood its dramatic difference and utilization in our everyday lives.

1. CREATE FLUID CONVERSATIONS.

You can find the high social intelligence persona at every party you attend. This person understands how to work the room, to talk to everyone to say appropriate things in order to be well liked by everyone. As a result, this person has high social expressiveness skills.

2. HOLD KNOWLEDGE OF APPROPRIATE SCRIPTS AND SOCIAL ROLES.

People with high social intelligence understand how to "play the game" of conversation, so to speak. They understand the appropriate rules and what must be said in the eyes of society customs. This fuels sophistication in any setting.

3. MAINTAIN HEIGHTENED LISTENING SKILLS.

People with high social intelligence have excellent listening skills. As a result of these heightened listening skills, people are able to feel like they connect well—that the person with high social intelligence actually heard, understood, and empathized with them. This is incredibly beneficial to fuel personal interaction.

4. COMPREHEND WHAT MAKES OTHER PEOPLE ANGRY.

People who have high social intelligence can read people well through linking to how these people are behaving and speaking. Generally speaking, people who do a lot of people watching are often good at this "reading of emotions." Note that if you understand how other people are thinking or what they are feeling, you can be better in-tune with what you should say to empathize in the conversation.

5. CREATE AN APPROPRIATE ROLE FOR YOURSELF.

People with high social intelligence can play many different roles, no matter the context in which that role is being played. Therefore, they can speak to many different people, no matter the social structure or their background. As a result of this ability, people with social intelligence can feel socially confident in any environment.

6. HOLD HIGH IMPRESSION MANAGEMENT SKILLS.

People with high social intelligence are continually concentrating on the various impressions they have on other people. They hold a balance between controlling the image they create for others of themselves and leaving these people an impression of their "true" selves. Therefore, they toe the line between being honest and controlling what they "present" to other people.

This can be very complex. But think about it this way: how many times have you felt that someone was phony, that someone was just trying to control the image you got of them? That person has not mastered this intricate balance of social intelligence. If that person was too honest about himself, however, you might hold a lack of respect for him. He might tell you things that disallow you to respect him. Therefore, a marriage of these two, honesty and preservation of sense of self, is essential for an appropriate level of social intelligence.

CHAPTER 3. HOW DO YOU DEVELOP SOCIAL INTELLIGENCE?

Social intelligence is one of the greatest elements you can utilize in order to live and thrive in your overarching society. You can read other people's behavior and understand how your own behavior influences other people. Through social intelligence, you can boost your internal well being, you can hold better conversations, you can create better personal relationships, and you can simply exist in this world with greater ease.

Look at the following example of social intelligence to better understand how it is orchestrated:

Your Friend or Acquaintance:

"Hey! I'm having a get-together this weekend. Would you be interested in coming?"

You, utilizing an engaging smile and curious, bright eyes:

"Are you having a birthday party?"

Doesn't this seem natural, paving the way toward further conversation and more questions and answers? During this orchestration, "you" have really wonderful social intelligence. But now, imagine the scenario differently:

Your Friend or Acquaintance:

"Hey! I'm having a get-together this weekend. Would you be interested in coming?"

You, without social intelligence, without any inflection, and without making eye contact; you appear disinterested and without amusement.

"What for?"

Do you see how in this instance, you "cut off" your friend and disallow future conversation? You don't look at him; you don't display interest in what he has to say. You simply respond without paying attention to your inflection or the way you maneuver your body.

This later interaction can develop an unfortunate misunderstanding between you and your friend. Ultimately, you could lose this friend, be deemed a "grump," and find yourself without any personal relationships.

Build a better social intelligence with the following techniques:

1. HOLD ETERNAL AWARENESS OF THE WAYS IN WHICH YOU COMMUNICATE WITHOUT WORDS.

What? Communicate without words?

That's right. Approximately ninety-three percent of all personal communication is non-verbal based. Therefore, everything you're doing with your body, every way in which you're inflecting your voice infects how you communicate what you're trying to say.

Therefore, consider your body language. When you speak to people, are you leaning into them, are you facing toward them, and are you engaging with them, physically? If not, if you're facing away from them, if you're gazing into the distance, or if you're frowning in some way, you could make them think you're disinterested or even angry with them. This creates an environment of misunderstanding.

Furthermore, you can't allow an outside force to alter your tone of voice. For example, if you're upset about your job and you speak forcibly to someone as a result of this job, you have just altered the way that person perceives you. Don't allow your emotions to get the best of your vocal inflections.

2. HONE ASSERTIVENESS SKILLS.

When you're beginning to develop social intelligence, it is important to hone your assertiveness by reflecting back on the responses other people have had to your actions.

When you assert yourself more readily, you are doing so in a way that offers the thoughts you have, the feelings you have, and what you want, without appearing like an aggressive person. You are not trying to force other people to do what you want. Rather—you are asserting how you feel and who you are. You are not wishy-washy, but you are not forceful, either.

Note that you can utilize these assertiveness skills to show how much you care for other people, to allow them to understand your deepest, most intimate feelings, and to show how much you want to excel in a company. This can be more natural for some than others. Never allow your low level of social intelligence to force people not to think you don't care for them. Never allow your low level of social intelligence to force people not to think of you for a promotion. Always allow people to understand what you're thinking and feeling—when it's appropriate—on a polite and respectful level.

3. TURN TO SOCIAL INTELLIGENCE BOTH ON THE INTERNET AND IN "REAL LIFE."

Generally, this book articulates the importance of social intelligence in the "offline" sphere. And this seems appropriate, given that the Internet offers a safe space for people lacking in physical social intelligence. The platform allows for people to think about what they want to say and articulate it with specific language that hones their emotions and their overarching point.

However, it's important to note that people can be rash on the Internet. People can be rash in emails to bosses, to friends, to partners. Always think about what you write and make sure you understand how it could be perceived. The words should not be confrontational or wishy-washy. Misunderstanding can often be rampant on the Internet. Keep things streamlined and understood.

4. DON'T ALLOW ONE MISUNDERSTANDING TO LEAD TO ANOTHER (AND ANOTHER).

Think about it. If you accidentally yield an inappropriate "meaning" to what you say—like, if you frown, even though you mean well when you say something—you could lead someone to retort back to you.

As a result of this retort, you could become incredibly frustrated. Confused. Angry at this person for responding to you in this way. This person misunderstood what you meant; as a result, the misunderstandings are going to continue because the anger has escalated to a new level.

Therefore, instead of creating a cycle, orchestrate something like the following:

"So. We're meeting at six then?" You say this with an irritated expression on your face. You're frowning; you seem like you don't really want to go. This is not the meaning you want to orchestrate. Rather, you do want to go, you are just preoccupied with something your girlfriend told you at lunch. (Doesn't this happen to you all the time?)

Your friend is confused at your sudden despondence. It seems like you don't want to meet up with him. As a result, he says, sarcastically, "Well. You don't have to go if you don't want to." He frowns, as well, because he is mirroring back what you're already created for him.

You have two choices here. You can either respond in anger, taking this to mean that your friend doesn't actually want you to meet up with him later. Or, you can respond in a way that refutes the misunderstanding cycle in its tracks.

Say something like this, with a clear, happy, and positive expression on your face:

"No, no. Of course I want to come! I'm sorry. I was just thinking about something else for a moment. I really want to see you later. And I don't be so messed in the head later, either." Make a joke of the misunderstanding; allow them to understand you're completely committed to seeing them later. This way, the incident passes easily.

5. CREATE AN AUTHENTIC EXCHANGE.

When you speak to people, as mentioned previously, it is essential to create an honest, appropriate impression of yourself. You cannot manipulate anyone as you speak; you must hold integrity.

In order to articulate this intricate art of creating an honest, appropriate image, look to the following techniques.

THE INTRICATE ART OF CREATING AN HONEST, APPROPRIATE IMPRESSION

As mentioned previously, one of the most important aspects of social intelligence involves "impression management skills."

But this is one of the most difficult aspects of social intelligence. After all, we all attempt to impress others, all the time. We try to get people to like us on a level that is not always honest. We say, for example, that we like things we don't really like. We attempt to talk about things we don't really know anything about.

So: how can you control how you are perceived by others—allow them to understand that you are intelligent, funny, well-liked, etc.—without seeming inauthentic? How can you appear like a successful person without appearing like a "faux" successful person?

Look to the following tips to better orchestrate your next conversation:

1. HAVE GREATER SELF-AWARENESS.

It is so important to know yourself and have high self-awareness in order to create an authentic persona. Note that this sort of challenges the initial idea of social intelligence—that we all must play many different roles, depending on the context or the social environment surrounding us. However, we must understand who we are on an intimate level, what our values are, and what we stand for, in order to articulate our individuality.

2. HOLD THOUGHTFULNESS AND PRUDENCY.

When we listen to other people, it is essential that we engage our brains and zone into the interactions. Our listening must bring us to an understanding about the other person's point of view. We must continually understand the consequence of our actions and what we say during these conversations as these elements can dramatically alter what occurs in the rest of the conversation. Be careful not to divulge too much information, too quickly.

3. HOLD MASTERY OF YOUR EMOTIONS.

It is important to hold your emotions tightly in your hand. You must control them throughout the entire dialogue. If you have an emotional outburst—become angry or sad quickly—you will create a negative impression of yourself. Note that emotions are an important element when linking with other people. However, regulating those emotions is incredibly important on the road to creating an environment of respect.

Note that all negative emotions, especially, like irritation, anger, or disgust, should be evoked with strategy. You can allow other people to know your displeasure, but only at appropriate times.

4. ALWAYS UPHOLD APPROPRIATE ETIQUETTE RULES.

Note that society holds many norms that bring a sort of "step-by-step" etiquette to a regular conversation or social situation. First and foremost, it is essential that you are polite during all stages of the conversation.

5. HOLD ETERNAL COURAGE.

Note that in order to orchestrate an appropriate impression, you must have a good deal of courage. This occurs most readily when you must strike a conversation with a stranger, for example, or assist someone in trouble. Sometimes, this courage must appear when you have to stand up for your internal convictions. When you stand up for these convictions, you are showing a level of honesty that many people will respect.

6. CREATE POSITIVITY.

Research shows clearly that people who are positive versus people who are negative have greater effect and have a better impression, overall. Smile. Be optimistic in conversation.

Note that creating an authentic, real, and honest impression on the people in your life can be incredibly difficult. Continue to practice the above strategies in order to display a persona that is both honest and controlled. Only then can you uphold the truest sense of social intelligence.

HOW TO DEVELOP A RAPPORT

What is rapport?

Essentially, rapport is something that occurs during conversation when everything you say, do, or think occurs in near synchronization with the person to whom you speak. Communication, then, churns from your unconscious mind to your friend's unconscious mind. Rapport offers the closest link, essentially, between two minds. It allows your brains to become, nearly, one unit. Note that we will discuss something similar to this in the next section, when we learn about mirror neurons and how those mirror neurons create a "single unit" of unconscious minds at the office.

Rapport creates an environment of mutual trust. As such, one of the first steps to developing a successful conversation and exhibiting social intelligence is honing your ability to develop a rapport with someone else. When you develop this rapport, you are exhibiting a sense of empathy toward this other person; you are showing him or her that you understand him, you empathize with his situation, and that the conversation can continue flowing in any direction—you're right there with him. Essentially, you're taking away any barriers that might otherwise have appeared in the conversation. You're allowing the other person—and yourself—to feel calm.

UNDERSTANDING HOW TO BUILD A RAPPORT WITH MATCHING

When attempting to build this rapport with another person, it is essential that you blend your beliefs ever so slightly. Note that this shouldn't, of course, completely detract from "who you are" on a personal level. Rather, it should bend just a bit toward the perspective of the person with whom you speak. Try to see life from his point of view.

An example of this talk is found when you meet someone, for example, at a bar and you're both watching the same game on the television. This person you meet is an Englishman who absolutely loves soccer—or his version of football. Because the World Cup is on the television screen, you're naturally discussing it. You grew up on American football; you love everything about it, and you have no use for soccer. However, because you're speaking to this Englishman before you, you need to ramp up your excitement for soccer in order to create a rapport. When you simply try to feel the excitement this Englishman feels about the game, something scary can occur. You can actually step into the shoes of the person next to you and become a small part of that Englishman. Your perceptions become altered, ever so slightly.

When you do this, you are utilizing a technique called matching. This is different than another technique called mirroring. When you mirror someone, you create an unconscious, precise mirror of this person; when you match him, however, you simply communicate as yourself—without becoming that other person—but still matching how he thinks, how he feels.

For example, when you speak to someone, you automatically want to "match" this person's tone. IF you're at a funeral, you'll naturally match the more somber tone of your friend or relative. However, you wouldn't mirror this tonality. For example, if you're a man, you wouldn't precisely mirror the way your younger niece talks. But your tone would "match" the tone of your younger niece, even though you wouldn't be talking like a young girl.

In much the same way, you would "match" the tone of the Englishman as he excitedly talks about soccer. But you wouldn't mirror his tone. If you were American, you wouldn't start speaking British English. You would develop a rapport by meeting him with a matched amount of energy.

LEARNING TO BUILD A BETTER RAPPORT

Note that when you're attempting to build a better rapport, it is essential to remember that tonality accounts for approximately thirty-eight percent of human-to-human conversation, and physiology accounts for approximately fifty-five percent of all communication. As such, you must account always for the way you say things, how you move your head, how you move your hands—how you do everything—on top of the important, precise words you chose.

What a nightmare, right?

Look to the following tips to better understand how to build a rapport and fuel a path to greater social intelligence.

1. Learn how to match the person with whom you speak. When you match, you allow the other person to think you're "like" him, even if you're not. You attempt to align your perceptions with this other person to yield a more streamlined conversation. You work further to align your physiology, your tonality, and your words with this person. Use the words he's using. If he says awesome, you say awesome.

2. Sit if this person is sitting. Slouch if this person is slouching. Stand if this person is standing. Get on the same level with this person to bring a level of compatibility to your relationship.

3. Mirror the other person's facial expressions. Note that your human face—and his—has fifty-three muscles that create essential subtleties, every day. Note if the person has a clenched jawline. Does this mean he's on edge? Note if this person has raised eyebrows. Is he curious? Continually match and understand his facial expressions to give yourself greater social intelligence.

HOW TO TELL IF YOU HAVE A RAPPORT

If you're having trouble understanding if you have a rapport with someone, if you're having trouble noting if you've built an environment of understanding, look to the following list to comprehend what the notion of rapport "feels like."

1. Feeling of internal, bodily warmth. This could be as simple as "butterflies in your stomach."

2. Noting that the other person blushes. This shows you that their cortisol levels—or their stress hormone levels—are decreasing fast. They feel calm in front of you. You're building a rapport.

3. You are able to switch from "pacing" along with this person—or following along, matching this person—to leading this person. Therefore, this person begins to match and mirror you instead of the other way around.

Building an appropriate rapport is one of the most essential ways to strengthen your social intelligence. Learn to speak to your peers, to your boss, to your co-workers, to your friends, and to your family members. Allow them to note that you care, that you can keep up with them on an emotional level, and that you can be turned to for anything. This way, you will create an environment of care and respect.

CHAPTER 4. THE ESSENTIAL LINK BETWEEN SOCIAL INTELLIGENCE AND LEADERSHIP

In 1998, a man named Daniel Goleman published a study on the link between emotional intelligence and leadership. Through this study, he asked the question: "what makes a leader?" and proceeded to comprehend the essential vitality of self-knowledge and empathy when it comes to leadership. (After all, being able to emotionally comprehend both one's self and others is incredibly important in the leadership field.) Since then, however, broadened research in this intricate study—the study of what happens inside of your brain when you have social interactions—has brought us to better understand how social intelligence links with leadership.

Of course, having social skills and being a leader is not a new link to make. In 1920, Edward Thorndike, who was the Columbia University psychologist at the time, noted that the best technical man in his field could fail as a result of his poor social intelligence. Therefore, "mechanical" intelligence was not the main, overarching factor in success versus failure. There was something else—the ways in which this person interacted with others—that really structured his success or his failure.

But what's new about the link between social intelligence and leadership?

WHAT YOU NEED TO KNOW IS THIS:

Things that natural-born leaders do, like understand other people's moods and show their empathetic feelings, affect their followers on a brain chemistry-level. Researchers note that the follower and the leader brain are actually both consciously and unconsciously linked. The minds become, in a sense, one greater system working toward one common goal.

The researchers note that the leader is the one that is able to "flip the switch," essentially, and bring all these brains together in a single unit. This leader has a better interior brain connectedness, as well, leading researchers to note that this leader is at the opposite spectrum of the person on the autism spectrum.

Therefore, if you were able to understand which behaviors build that greater interconnectivity, that greater brain circuitry, you would be able to make yourself into a better leader. You would be able to sweep yourself further to the leader side of the spectrum, away from the autism spectrum, just by honing and strengthening your interior brain connectedness.

Therefore, the researchers noted that in order to become the best possible leader you can be, you must find actual interest and care for the positive generation of your followers. You must love what you're doing in order to build that connectivity.

UNDERSTAND THAT PEOPLE SHADOW THEIR LEADERS

Recently, neuroscientists have discovered something called mirror neurons. These neurons mimic what another person does.

This was discovered the following, ever-interesting way.

Italian scientists were studying a monkey's brain. One day, an Italian scientist was eating an ice cream cone. (As they so often do.) He lifted the ice cream cone to his mouth. Just then, one of these neurons was activated in the monkey's brain. The monkey's brain was experiencing, on some level, what the Italian researcher was experiencing. The brain cells are sort of like Wi-Fi cells. They both unconsciously and consciously understand other people's emotions and they reflect these emotions. Therefore, in a sense, the monkey and the man shared the experience of the ice cream.

This relationship is heightened when it comes to the follower and the leader. Essentially, the follower is more in-tune with the leader's emotions. The leader's actions and emotions activate the followers to do certain things, to act in certain ways.

Look to the following case study that exhibits how these neurons interact in followers when they received feedback from their leaders.

There were two groups of "followers." One group of people received negative feedback for their performance. However, during the negative feedback "performance" delivered by the leaders, the leaders smiled at them. They acted positively toward them. They performed the negative feedback as if they were delivering positive feedback. They activated these "feel good" neurons in the followers' minds.

The other group, on the other hand, received positive feedback in a negative manner. Therefore, the words were "yes" but the frowns and the shaking of heads screamed "no." The activation of these feel-good neurons did not take place.

In the end, the two groups were asked how they did. The people who had received negative feedback with a positive, encouraging performance felt better about their time than the people who had received positive feedback with a negative performance.

Therefore, if leaders strive for excellence in their people, in their followers, it is essential that they demand better abilities from their people—with a positive demeanor about them. This strengthens these core, mirror neurons and builds an environment of positivity.

HAPPY, SUCCESSFUL MOODS WITH POSITIVE NEURAL FEEDBACK

It's incredible to learn that there is an entire portion of your mirror neurons that are only activated and working when you see smiles or hear laughter. Therefore, if you have a boss that scares you—a boss who doesn't make you laugh, who makes you frown—these neurons are never activated at work. You are, therefore, continually putting forth a sub-par performance at no fault of your own. However, if you have a boss that brings ease to your work environment, your work environment triggers a follower-group that yields good performance. These followers can perform above and beyond—simply because they feed from the mirror neurons activated in their brains.

THE BLUNT BOSS

Let's look at the following story to get a better sense for the disastrous notion of a boss lacking in empathy and social intelligence—and what you can do if this person is you.

Consider Rachel. Rachel is a marketing manager at a large-scale company. She has a brilliant track record. She's a forward, strategic thinker. She is able to make goals and meet them. In the hiring manager's eye, Rachel is the best person for the job.

However, after just six months in the managing position, Rachel is a mess. She is aggressive and overly opinionated. And why shouldn't she be? She's the best at what she does. However, she is very careless about what she says and how she says it. She's downright mean, sometimes, to both her followers and to higher people on the totem pole. Clearly, something needs to change.

Rachel's boss calls in a psychologist to better evaluate this floundering leader. The psychologist gives Rachel an evaluation as she maneuvers through her day. As a result, Rachel receives very low scores based on her service orientation, her empathy, her ability to manage internal and external conflicts, and her flexibility. The psychologist then leaves to speak with the people who work most often with Rachel on a daily basis. Each person states that Rachel is unable to create a rapport, to speak at ease. She can't understand other people's emotions; she can't understand when she is being too aggressive or assertive. Her boss and her boss' boss are becoming incredibly irritated with her. She might lose her job.

Suddenly, Rachel understands that her job is on the line, especially as a result of the feedback she receives from the psychologist. She finally realizes that all of her desires for the company and for her employees are not being understood.

Therefore, Rachel begins to analyze her everyday encounters with people. She analyzes the things she tries to initiate—the conversations in which she asks certain things of employees—and she analyzes which ones fail and which ones are successful. When she understands this on an intimate level, she is finally able to comprehend which way she should speak with employees—which way works best for both her and the employee. She begins to understand how other people perceive her, and she works to better herself, to fuel herself with enhanced positivity, and to become more sophisticated in everyday interactions.

As a result of these alterations, Rachel begins to bring an enhanced social circuitry in her brain. She begins to build neural connections like one would build muscles.

Rachel transforms gradually but permanently. She becomes a different sort of person, a different sort of leader.

As a result, we find the following conclusion:

Your behavior can develop different neural pathways. You can build yourself into whatever type of person you want to be, depending on the ways in which you act and speak. You are not a slave to what has happened to you, what your personality is, or what your genes are. You can learn to be however you want to be.

SOCIAL INTELLIGENCE, LEADERS, AND CRISIS SITUATIONS

Note that the work environment automatically brings a surge of the stress hormones cortisol and adrenaline. When cortisol pulses in your system at lower, pace levels, your ability to process thoughts is in its top gear. Therefore, pressure that exerts this low level of cortisol is actually essential on your path to greater success.

However, when a leader creates an enormous surge of cortisol, your mind is unable to focus. You are unable to remember anything, plan anything, or exhibit the intellect you know you have.

Therefore, there's a science behind "pushing" your employees, especially if you are a leader. You must understand them, give them positive feedback, but always give them an extra push toward the eternal goal. Only then will they have the appropriate level of cortisol in their system to fuel them toward the extra mile. Only then will they look to you, mirror your positive and fighting image, and work toward an appropriate end result. Only then will you find your leadership skills undeniably successful.

CHAPTER 5. RAISING CHILDREN WITH SOCIAL INTELLIGENCE

Note that no matter how often you scrutinize your children, look under their noses, clean their scrapes, know every inch of their bodies, they're looking at you even closer. You are what they know of the world. You must create an environment of social intelligence via what you do and what you say.

Raising children in an environment of enhanced social intelligence is one of the most essential ways to build a better future world. Note that everything you show your children, via your reactions to things, your moods, your actions, and your facial expressions, will ultimately be mirrored in your children. You must be continually aware of how you're perceived. When you show them the best version of yourself, when you show them who you are on an honest level, you're allowing your children to better understand themselves on an intimate level. You are nurturing them in an environment of understanding.

Turn to the following four best techniques to create children with enhanced social intelligence. When you teach them social intelligence early, you are eliminating the possibility that they will be bullies in the future. You are giving them greater capabilities at work, at school, and in their chosen careers. You are giving them a path to greater success.

1. BEGIN OPEN COMMUNICATION EARLY.

When your baby is born, begin speaking to him. Begin your personal relationship, your two-way conversation, even before your baby speaks English. Speak to your baby in a respectful manner that allows him to understand that he his human, that he is respected.

Note that babies have an ability to comprehend what you're saying to them far before they can distinguish different words. (After all, only seven percent of all communication is language-based.) Always tell them what you're doing, what they're about to do, and what's going on in the world around them. When you begin doing this early, you'll discover that in a few years, they understood you the whole time. You allowed them to participate early through facial expressions, through burps, through however they are able to communicate. You are giving them a dialogue before anyone else, and you are allowing them to be heard.

2. STAY HONEST.

So often, parental guidelines suggest utilizing games, tricks, distractions, punishments, or rewards in order to fuel an environment of education for children. However, these things don't build social intelligence. They instead promote inauthenticity and shame, especially in the case of punishment.

Remember that everything you do is automatically "trumped" by the way in which you're acting while you do it. Therefore, if you're attempting to play a game but you're acting like you're in a bad mood, your child is going to pick up on the bad mood and remember the bad mood—not what she learned during the game.

Therefore, always be direct and sincere, just as you would be to any adult. Your child deserves it.

3. MODEL THE BEST VERSION OF YOURSELF.

Always administer direct and polite communication to your children, no matter their age. Tell them you made a mistake when you did, even if your child is a baby. Always show your children an enhanced level of empathy, forgiveness, patience, etc. Your children will pick up on them if they see you show them, as well.

Also, show and tell your feelings, when you can. Your children will note if you're upset about something, about anything, and they'll appreciate knowing the reasons why you're upset.

4. UNDERSTAND THAT PRACTICE MAKES PERFECT.

Note that your children need a space to practice their social intelligence. After all, society and social cues take a long time to "pick up." (Many of us are still struggling, after all.) Therefore, allow your young children, even your babies, to interact with people their own age. Babies begin to learn from each other very early.

Furthermore, it's important that you don't interfere in your child's play. (You can play with your baby and your child, but make sure that you allow him or her to make up the rules. It's his world, after all!)

Further note that children, especially toddler-aged children, have undeniable conflicts. However, if you allow your children to resolve their conflicts on their own—

without interfering—you are allowing them to build their social intelligence in amazing ways.

Acknowledge that your children have feelings, just as you acknowledge your own feelings. Treat your children's feelings as you would your own—in an environment of respect. Build a new era of children that reap the rewards of social intelligence, and eliminate bullying and inability to solve conflicts.

Your child can truly begin exercising their social intelligence muscles at this early age. This way, they'll be ahead of the curve when they enter into their schools, their jobs, and their careers as enhanced, understanding, and empathetic adults.

CHAPTER 6. SOCIAL INTELLIGENCE: A CONCLUSION

Social intelligence is absolutely essential in order to create an environment of understanding, of empathy, of leadership, and of camaraderie. Because understanding of social intelligence was not strong when you were a child, your parents were not conscious of the social intelligence they created for you in your home environment. Therefore, they probably did not display a world of social intelligence via what they said to you, what they did around you, how they displayed their feelings, and how they showed you what they were thinking via their facial alterations and their tonality.

Therefore, in this adult world with the renewed vitality and understanding of social intelligence, it is essential that you begin to strengthen your interactions, you abilities, and your social intelligence in order to be the best possible version of yourself in both your relationships and your career.

With social intelligence, you can succeed by showing respect and conversational versatility in the workplace. You can deliver yourself with honesty and with assertiveness, allowing other people to know who you are, what your values are, and what you want to do with your life. With social intelligence, you can maximize each sentence, each moment, and each next-step in your life.

Learn to utilize social intelligence to make the most of every minute, create a plethora of unique and deep relationships, and discover who you are on an intimate level.

ABOUT THE AUTHOR

The mission of Jonny Bell is to be able to help inspire and change the world, one reader at a time.

This author wants to provide the most amazing life tools that anyone can apply into their lives. It doesn't matter whether you have hit rock bottom in your life or your life is amazing and you want to keep taking it to another level.

If you are like this writer, then you are probably looking to become the best version of yourself. You are likely not to settle for an okay life. You want to live an extraordinary life. Not only to be filled within but also to contribute to society.

He has been studying and applying psychology for over 5 years and met a lot of interesting people along the way. With these writings, Bell wants to keep inspiring others to change for the better.

OTHER BOOKS BY JONNY BELL

Sociology: A Practical Understanding of Why We Do What We Do

Emotional Intelligence: A Practical Guide to Mastering Emotions: Emotions Handbook and Journal

Cognitive Behavioral Therapy: CBT Essentials and Fundamentals: A Practical Guide to CBT and Modern Psychology

Social Psychology: Essentials and Fundamentals: A Practical Guide to Social Psychology and Sociology

Applied Psychology: Practical Guide to the Human Mind, Step-by-Step Advice to the Understandings of Psychology

Sports Psychology: Inside the Athlete's Mind: High Performance - Sports Psychology for Athletes and Coaches

Positive Psychology: Research and Applications of the Science of Happiness and Fulfillment: New Field, New Insights

Spirituality: A Practical Guide to Spiritual Awakening: A Journey of Self-Awareness and Spiritual Growth

FREE PREVIEW OF

POSITIVE PSYCHOLOGY:

Research and Applications of the Science of Happiness and Fulfillment

NEW FIELD, NEW INSIGHTS

JONNY BELL

Copyright © 2014 by Jonny Bell

WHY YOU SHOULD READ THIS BOOK

This book will help you understand a revolutionary branch of psychology: positive psychology. Positive psychology, jolting from the traditional, depressing psychologies of day's past, prescribes the ways in which you can find true, internal satisfaction. It no longer lingers upon what is wrong with you; instead, it pushes you to ask: what is right with me and how can I improve upon that? How can I utilize my talents in order to maximize my life while I'm living it and achieve true self-satisfaction. You can be happy in the face of adversity and stress. You can push beyond lack of confidence, pessimism, and helplessness in order to achieve your goals and reach self-actualization? The book outlines research-driven concepts to allow true happiness to implant itself in your life. It quantifies decades of understanding about what makes humans happy or unhappy, and lands with a firm grasp on: yourself.

CHAPTER 1. COMPREHENDING POSITIVE PSYCHOLOGY

Positive Psychology: the new psychology revolution swooping through the world, is asking the most interesting question: how can one be happy? Positive Psychology is the inverse of what is traditionally termed "regular" psychology. While regular psychology works to rectify psychological problems, to instill hearty, better mental states after mental trauma, positive psychology works to build positivity and satisfaction in normal life. The swerve from mental instability psychology to positive psychology is relatively recent; the interest in health and mental growth churned to the scene sometime in the past half century after many years of pegging people into mental institutions and studying their brains. Why not study the brain of a health person and try to scientifically administer greater health and happiness upon that person's life? Why not work to discover the ways in which a person can work toward a better, more fulfilling life? These are the general questions behind the exciting new field.

POSITIVE VERSUS THE NEGATIVE

Essentially, the "regular" psychology school's focus upon faltering human development doesn't tell the entire story of a person's brain life. Simply knowing what occurs in the brain after stress, after schizophrenia has kicked in, or after emotional trauma has occurred lends the view of a ruptured brain. One can completely understand how a "ruptured brain" works—or ultimately falters on a cellular, minute level. But how can one understand the ruptured brain without paying attention to a full, hearty brain? The full, hearty brain begins with all of its "pieces" in place: that is, it's healthy, full of vibrancy. Nothing is going wrong. However, most brains start out in this normal state. Something: life experience, choice, or environment triggers the brain to ultimately falter or reach to great, happy heights. The topic of positive psychology, then, tries to study the happy, healthy brain in order to help other brains to reach this magnificent, positive balance. Just as traditional psychology works to rectify a faltering brain, positive psychology works to push the brain forward: to ultimate life and joy.

THE OVER-ARCHING GOAL OF POSITIVE PSYCHOLOGY

The ultimate goal of positive psychology on a personal-level is, essentially, to learn the ways in which one can think through the neuron path to joyful emotions. Negative thoughts—on a drastic level—lead to brain disorders and counter-intuitive living. Therefore, positive psychology provides the idea that positive thoughts lead to brain growth and fulfillment. Of course, these positive thoughts—brought on a very person-level—vary from person to person. Not all emotions are the same.

Furthermore, "positive emotions" are not meant to completely eliminate negative emotions. Human beings have immense subtlety; basic positive emotions are swayed and "colored in" by gray, negative emotions.

Think of an example: a person achieves great success and graduates from a university. One would think that this person feels the utmost satisfaction at the graduation ceremony: after all, he's worked through many achievements and had to think positively for many years in order to reach this goal. However, for very personal, environmental reasons, his graduation ceremony may be "colored in" by a negative emotion. For example, his father could have died the previous year, therefore missing out on his graduation and lending him feelings of sadness. This does not work against the feeling of joy he feels for graduating; instead, this negative emotion fills out the satisfactory feeling, giving it a complete, human edge. Despite the unhappiness he feels, he still feels immense joy. It's complicated: but what involving humans isn't complex?

THE THREE ISSUES OF POSITIVE PSYCHOLOGY

Positive psychology looks to three main issues during its research and analysis of the human brain and body.

POSITIVE EMOTIONS

Positive emotions study the ways in which a person is happy and content with one's past events, happy in one's present situation, and hopeful for one's future. Therefore, one can feel pleasure from these three sectors. One can remember things that happened in the past and feel joy; alternately, past events can haunt a person, causing unfortunate mental blockings on the road to happiness. One can feel happiness from the hope one feels for the future. This can range from big ideas to small ideas. One can be happy about Christmas around the corner or fueled with the passion to study law in the coming years at a major university. Either of these situations brings hopeful joy. Present joy varies from day to day, obviously, based on current environmental factors. Positive psychology studies the ways in which one's present environment works against or fuels a happy mindset. It studies the ways in which the present brings satisfaction.

POSITIVE INDIVIDUAL TRAITS

Positive individual trait studies in the field of positive psychology lend an understanding of the ways in which a person's talents bring satisfaction and life joy. These talents could be natural: the ability to sing or dance, for example. They could be fueled by one's work environment: the talents one brings to the office in order to write the next big news story or work through the goals of the company. Everyone has inner strengths, inner virtues to push them toward a better, more fulfilling life. Not everyone uses these strengths and virtues wisely. Many are wasted.

POSITIVE INSTITUTIONS

The positive institution methods are based upon the strengths and virtues that stem from various institutions in one's life. These institution-led strengths bring joy and fulfillment to a community of people—providing a unit of safety and inclusion throughout a group. This, essentially, brings a level of relationship joy and satisfaction. It provides something to reflect one's self upon: one can compare one's self to the satisfaction of the community. If the community is fulfilled, provided with institutions that lend fulfilling relationships, one can assimilate into this environment and prosper.

CHAPTER 2. HISTORY OF POSITIVE PSYCHOLOGY

Understand the intricate history of positive psychology and the great waves it has created in the past fifteen years.

THE EARLY AND MID TWENTIETH CENTURY

Prior to the Second World War, psychology worked much like it does today: it worked to cure all mental diseases via mental hospitals and therapists; it worked to provide fulfilling and satisfactory lives for patients; and it worked to identify high talent and further that talent's way into the greater world.

Unfortunately, the years after World War II changed everything. Psychology became primarily cure-based. Therefore, there wasn't a sense to improve something that wasn't already broken. This could have been a result of the war; the nation had been through great traumas, and improving that which had been broken was on the minds of everyone. Abnormal behavior and mental illnesses had to be squashed. Post-traumatic stress disorder (PTSD) hadn't been recognized yet; however, psychologists knew the tragedy of war on the human brain in a very broad sense. They worked to repair it.

Abraham Maslow

During these subsequent "abnormality-focused" years after World War II, a few psychologists chose to focus on humanistic psychology. Abraham Maslow was one of these driving forces, one of the first in the game.

While working alongside Gestalt psychologist Max Wertheimer and Ruth Benedict, an anthropologist at Brooklyn College, Maslow was incredibly alert. He found both Benedict and Wertheimer to be exceptional: highly attuned to themselves, to their happiness, and to their careers. He later took note of their sure happiness and success as he cultivated his humanistic psychology.

Abraham Maslow created theories about self-actualization, peak experiences, and hierarchy of needs.

The hierarchy of needs displays five stages that a man must attain in order to focus on his internal happiness. One must first maintain one's biological health; afterwards, one can find safety, a place to call one's home, relationships, self-esteem fulfillment, and—ultimately—self-actualization.

Self-Actualization: Maslow's Theory

Self-Actualization, one of Maslow's humanistic psychology theories, prescribes the idea that what a man can become, he must become. If he has met the other four stages of the hierarchy of needs and sees his potential laid out before him, he must reach that potential. It is the idea that one can become more full, more complete in one's self.

Self-actualization affects people in incredible ways, according to Maslow's theory. Self-actualized people take joy in solving problems in the greater, external world: problems that don't involve them. They feel a sense of personal responsibility. It allows for a deep sense of appreciation; self-actualized people see the world around them with a sharp eye, every-understanding that their lives are incredible, that each experience brings a sense of wonder.

Furthermore, self-actualized people reap the rewards of solitude. They enjoy their human relationships, of course; after all, relationships lie on the third step of the hierarchy of needs. However, the self-actualized person needs a few hours to breathe by himself every single day. This way, he can focus on who he wants to be and meeting their full potential.

The self-actualized person further reaches another one of Maslow's theories. He reaches peak experiences. The peak experience is a moment of ecstasy: one cannot fully grasp the intense joy one fells during these experiences. It is a moment of pure bliss. Afterwards, one feels completely rejuvenated and electrified. These peak experiences actually inspire one to further one's life, to reach for greater self-actualization.

Abraham Maslow's work is incredibly important; he pushed the limits of psychology from the 1950's mainstream, abnormal-focused realms. His theories are currently widely accepted with the resurgence of positive psychology.

MARTIN SELIGMAN AND THE RESURGENCE OF POSITIVE PSYCHOLOGY

1998 brought the election of the new president of the American Psychological Association. Martin Seligman stepped up to the position, bringing with him a new psychology theme: positive psychology. He lent all the modern ideas currently utilized and researched today: that the mind can ultimately decide to be joyous and satisfied and happy. In 2009, just eleven years later, the first World Congress on Positive Psychology took the reigns in Philadelphia, allowing the world to understand the research and the explosion of life-affirming science currently pulsing from the realms of positive psychology. At the convention, Seligman was a featured speaker. These days, he is widely regarded as the ultimate father of positive psychology.

CHAPTER 3. POSITIVE PSYCHOLOGY RESEARCH ANALYSIS

Read more ...

Positive Psychology: Research and Applications of the Science of Happiness and Fulfillment: New Field, New Insights

ONE LAST THING...

If you enjoyed this book or found it useful I'd be very grateful if you'd post a short review on Amazon. Your support really does make a difference and I read all the reviews personally so I can get your feedback and make this book even better.

Thanks again for your support!

Made in the USA
Middletown, DE
30 April 2016